✔ KU-166-483

8th June 2006

To:
Rach

From:
Sas x

God Made Us Sisters

Written and compiled by Conover Swofford

Illustrated by Katharine Barnwell

Designed by Arlene Greco

Inspire Books is an imprint of
Peter Pauper Press, Inc.

For permissions please see
the last page of this book.

Text copyright © 1999
Peter Pauper Press, Inc.
202 Mamaroneck Avenue
White Plains, NY 10601
Illustrations copyright © 1999
Katharine Barnwell
ISBN 0-88088-124-0
Printed in China
21 20 19 18 17 16

Visit us at www.peterpauper.com

God Made Us Sisters

God made us sisters

Because He knew

How close we would be—

Me and you.

I thank my God
every time I remember you.

Philippians 1:3 NIRV

*F*or there is no friend like a sister

In calm or stormy weather.

Christina Rossetti

A sister is a friend who has shared her life with you.

Sometimes a sister loves you
better than you love yourself.

I am never alone—
I always have you,
my sister.

*B*lest be the tie that binds

Our hearts . . .

We share our mutual woes,

Our mutual burdens bear;

And often for each other flows

The sympathizing tear.

John Fawcett

A ministering angel

shall my sister be.

William Shakespeare

*W*hat a beautiful thought—

we are sisters!

*M*ay God use us
to show the world the
true meaning of sisters.

*I*t is right for me to feel

this way about . . . you.

I love you with

all my heart.

Philippians 1:7 NIRV

*M*ay the Lord look

on you with favor

and give you his peace.

Numbers 6:26 NIRV

*T*here is no love

like the love between sisters.

*T*he appreciation of your

sister grows with age.

*T*hose who love God

must also love

their . . . sisters.

1 John 4:21 NIRV

May the LORD keep watch
between you and me when
we are away from each other.

Genesis 31:49 NIRV

*I*n every situation
through time without end,
I'm glad you're my sister
and glad you're my friend.

*S*isters are never
fair weather friends.
Sisters are
"all weather" friends.

I'm glad God gave

you the sisterly advice

so you can give it to me

when I need it.

God made us sisters
as part of His plan
that we each have a friend
and a helping hand.

I'm glad God's
plan for our lives included
making us sisters.

I pray that you may enjoy good health, and that all may go well with you.

3 John 2 NEB

I'm glad you're my sister—

it's a tough job,

but somebody

has to do it!

S eldom do we disagree

I ncredible as that seems

S o I know you are willing

T o understand my dreams

E ven when you try to

R estrain my wilder schemes!

*S*isters forever!—no matter how

hard you try to deny it!

*G*od created each of us out

of part of the other's heart.

*W*e share, we care,
we're always there.
We're sisters.

I always thank my God as I remember you in my prayers.

Philemon 4 NIV

*Y*our love has given me great
joy and encouragement.

Philemon 7 NIV

*Y*ou know when to listen
and when to talk;
you know when I need advice
and when I don't.
You're my sister.

*Y*our life is a blessing
not only to me but
to everyone who comes in
contact with you.

*F*aithful until the end—
my sister, my friend.

*Y*ou always want what's best
    for me.
I want what's best for you.
Together we show all the
    world
God's love between us two.

*Y*ou're never too busy
for me. That's what being
a sister is all about.

*Y*ou give to me the best
you have and I give
my best to you.

God gave us one another
to share life's ups and
    downs—
so one of us is serious;
the other one a clown.
We complement each other
(though some may think
    that odd).
Together hand in hand
    each day
we walk in the smile of God.

Slow to suspect—
    quick to trust,

Slow to condemn—
    quick to justify,

Slow to offend—
    quick to defend,

Slow to expose—
    quick to shield,

Slow to reprimand—
    quick to forbear,

Slow to belittle—
quick to appreciate,

Slow to demand—
quick to give,

Slow to provoke—
quick to conciliate,

Slow to hinder—
quick to help,

Slow to resent—
quick to forgive.

Herald of Holiness

*T*ogether we give people
a picture of how God
intended sisters to be.

*O*n the day that you were
born, God blessed me with
a lifelong friend.

*F*riends may come
and friends may go,
but a sister is forever.

I will bless those

who bless you.

Genesis 12:3 NKJV

*T*wo people are better
than one. They can help
each other in everything
they do.

Ecclesiastes 4:9 NIrV

God made us sisters
because our differences
complement each other.

Carry each other's burdens.

Galatians 6:2 NIV

*T*here are no debts

between sisters.

*T*he love of a sister is
stronger than friendship.

*L*et me stop and say,

"You're my sister.

I love you."

*I*f you're that smart,

I must be gorgeous!

Most of all,
love one another deeply.

1 Peter 4:8 NIrV

*D*o two walk

together unless they have

agreed to do so?

Amos 3:3 NIV

A sister sees the wild
imaginings of your heart
and manages to convince
herself and you that
they are beautiful dreams.

God gave me a sister

so I could know His love

here on earth.

I'm proud to claim

you as my sister

(even in public!).

Sisters share a bond that
nothing can break.

A sister never says
anything behind
your back that she wouldn't
say to your face.

*W*alk beside me,
my sister, down life's road
so that I can reach out and
touch your hand when I
need a hand to hold.

I have not stopped giving
thanks for you, remembering
you in my prayers.

Ephesians 1:16 NIV

A sister listens to your heart,
not just your words.

*B*e kind one to another,

tenderhearted, forgiving

one another.

Ephesians 4:32 NKJV

I love you.

You love me.

We're sisters

For eternity.

*I*t's a good thing we
don't keep track of all we
do for each other, because
if we did, we wouldn't have
time to do anything else!

*Y*ou are more

than my sister;

you are part of my heart.

*K*nowing you're my sister

makes my heart glow.

*H*aving a sister the same
size as yourself immediately
doubles your wardrobe.

hmmm!!
this one doesn't
quite work for us,
coz I'm a midget!!
:)

Definition of a sister:
Someone you can trust
with your secrets; who
will stand by you no matter
what; who always loves
and accepts you.

God made us sisters.
I'm glad we chose
to be friends.

*lots of love
from*

Sas
xxx